GAYATRI

GAYATRI

The Prayers & Remembrances of the Inayati Sufis

Including those of
the Inayati-Maimuni Sufis

Modern Reader's Edition

Hazrat Inayat Khan

Edited and Annotated by
Pir Netanel Miles-Yépez

The Inayati-Maimuni Order
Boulder, Colorado
2024

*"The old shall be renewed,
and the new shall be made holy."*
— Rabbi Avraham Yitzhak Kook

Copyright © 2024 Netanel Miles-Yépez
First edition. All rights reserved.

This book has been produced for the Inayati-Maimuni Order in cooperation with Albion-Andalus Books.

No part of this book may be reproduced or transmitted in any form or by any means, electronic or mechanical, including photocopy, recording, or any information storage or retrieval system, except for brief passages in connection with a critical review, without permission in writing from the publisher:

Albion-Andalus, Inc.
P. O. Box 19852
Boulder, CO 80308
www.albionandalus.com

Design and composition by Albion-Andalus Books
Cover design by D.A.M. Cool Graphics
Cover image: "Inayati-Maimuni Heart & Wings" by Netanel Miles-Yépez.
Mehndi design used from Vecteezy.com

ISBN-13: (HC) 978-1-953220-25-7

Manufactured in the United States of America

Toward the One
The Perfection of Love, Harmony, and Beauty
The Only Being
United with all the Illuminated Souls
Who form the Embodiment of the Message
The Spirit of Guidance

CONTENTS

Editor's Preface	ix
Morning Prayers	1
Mid-day Prayers	9
Evening Prayers	15
Occasional Prayers	19
Remembrances	27
Inayati-Maimuni Prayers & Remembrances	35
Notes	43
Biographies	48

Editor's Preface

The major prayers of Inayati Sufism are drawn from two works by Hazrat Inayat Khan, the *Gayan* and the *Vadan*. Both works have a section entitled "Gayatri," each containing prayers composed by Hazrat Inayat Khan. *Gāyatrī* in Sanskrit is literally, *trī*, 'that which gives deliverance,' and *gāya*, 'through singing.' A gifted Indian classical musician, Inayat Khan chose musical terms, such as "Boulas," "Ragas" and "Talas," to name many of the sections of these Sufi spiritual works.

This prayer book, also entitled *Gayatri*, includes all of the prayers in the "Gayatri" sections of the *Gayan* and *Vadan*, as well as other prayers and remembrances, composed by Hazrat Inayat Khan, held and honored in the tradition of Inayati Sufism. I have edited and adapted many of the original prayers and remembrances for clarity in modern English and made them gender inclusive (rather than using the masculine personal pronoun in an inclusive sense, as was the convention in Hazrat Inayat Khan's day). I have also added notes in the back to explain context, non-English vocabulary, or the origins of various prayers.

It should be remembered that the versions of the prayers and remembrances in this booklet are interpretations of the originals and open to error. I take full responsibility for any errors I have introduced. Please know that I have approached the material with the utmost respect and have only made changes to them in the hope that the updated language will help to spread the Message of God "far and wide." I encourage any readers who are new to them to acquaint themselves with the originals (which may be obtained from the various Inayati organizations) and learn the differences. It goes without saying that one should learn to recite the prayers in accordance with the custom of one's own community. These versions are only to give you options for use in your own personal prayer practice.

In addition to the prayers and remembrances of Hazrat Inayat Khan, I have also added a section of universalist prayers and remembrances of the Inayati-Maimuni Sufi community composed by myself and Pir-o-Murshid Zalman Sulayman Schachter-Shalomi, of blessed memory. These are included here for the use of that community.

Pir Netanel Mu'in ad-Din Miles-Yépez
Boulder, Colorado, December 31st, 2023

> "Happiness lies in thinking or doing
> That which one considers beautiful."
> — *The Bowl of Saqi*

MORNING PRAYERS

Invocation[1]

This is not my body;
This is the temple
Of the heart.

Toward the One[2]

Toward the One,
The Perfection of Love,
Harmony, and Beauty,
The Only Being,
United with all
The Illuminated Souls,
Who form
The Embodiment
Of the Master,
The Spirit of Guidance.

Saum[3]

Praise be to you,
God, most high,
Omnipotent,
Omnipresent,
All-pervading,
The only being.

Take us in Your
Parental arms,
Raise us from the
Denseness of the earth!

Your beauty
We do worship;
To You we
Willingly surrender.

Merciful and
Compassionate God,
Ideal sustainer
Of humanity,
You only
Do we worship,
And toward You alone
Do we aspire!

Open our hearts
Toward your beauty;
Illuminate our souls
With divine light.

O perfection of love,
Harmony and beauty,
All-powerful creator,
Sustainer, judge,
And forgiver
Of our shortcomings,
Sovereign God
Of the east
And of the west,
Of the worlds
Above and below,
Of the seen
And unseen beings,
Pour upon us your
Love and your light!

Gayatri

Give sustenance
To our bodies,
Hearts, and souls;
Use us for the purpose
That Your
Wisdom chooses;
Guide us on the path
Of your own goodness!

Draw us closer to You
In every moment
Of our lives,
Until in us is reflected
Your grace, your glory,
Your wisdom, your joy
And your peace!
Amen.

Your words flow
As the sacred river;
Your thought rises
As a divine spring,
Your tenderness
Awakens sympathy
In my heart!

Beloved Teacher,
Your very being
Is forgiveness.

The clouds of
Doubt and fear
Are scattered by your
Piercing glance.

All ignorance
Vanishes in your
Illuminating
Presence.

A new hope
Is born in my heart
As I breathe Your
Peaceful atmosphere!

Inspiring Guide
Through life's
Labyrinthine ways,
In you, I feel
An abundance
Of blessing!
Amen.

Remembrance

Recite eleven times:

Pour upon us Your
Love and your light!

Pir

Inspirer of my mind,
Consoler of my heart,
Healer of my spirit,
Your presence lifts me
From earth unto heaven!

Morning Prayers

silsila[5]

Recitation of the lineage:

Haz'rat Jibril

Haz'rat Muhammad,
Rasul Allah

Haz'rat 'Ali,
Wali Allah

Haz'rat Khwaja
Hasan Basri

Haz'rat Khwaja
'Abd al-Wahid bin Zayd

Haz'rat Khwaja
Fuzayl bin 'Ayaz

Haz'rat Khwaja
Ibrahim ibn Adham
Balkhi

Haz'rat Khwaja
Huzayfa Mar'ashi

Haz'rat Khwaja
Hubayra Basri

Haz'rat Khwaja
Mumshad 'Ulu Dinwari

Haz'rat Khwaja
Abu Ishaq Shami Chishti

Haz'rat Khwaja
Abu Ahmad Abdal Chishti

Haz'rat Khwaja
Abu Muhammad Chishti

Haz'rat Khwaja
Nasir ad-Din Abu Yusuf
Chishti

Haz'rat Khwaja
Qutb ad-Din Mawdud
Chishti

Haz'rat Khwaja
Hajji Sharif Zindani

Haz'rat Khwaja
'Usman Harvani

Haz'rat Khwaja
Mu'in ad-Din Hasan,
Gharib Nawaz,
Sanjari-Ajmiri

Haz'rat Khwaja
Qutb ad-Din Mas'ud,
Bakhtiyar Kaki

Haz'rat Khwaja
Farid ad-Din Mas'ud,
Ganj-i Shakar,
Ajhodani

GAYATRI

Haz'rat Khwaja Nizam ad-Din *Awliya'*, *Mahbub-i Ilahi*, Badauni

Haz'rat Khwaja Nasir ad-Din Mahmud, *Chiragh-i Dihli*

Haz'rat Shaykh al-Mashaykh Kamal ad-Din *'Allama*

Haz'rat Shaykh al-Mashaykh Siraj ad-Din

Haz'rat Shaykh al-Mashaykh Ilm ad-Din

Haz'rat Shaykh al-Mashaykh Mahmud Rajan

Haz'rat Shaykh al-Mashaykh Jamal ad-Din Jamman

Haz'rat Shaykh al-Mashaykh Hasan Muhammad

Haz'rat Shaykh al-Mashaykh Muhammad A'zam

Haz'rat Shaykh al-Mashaykh Yahya Madani

Haz'rat Shaykh al-Mashaykh Shah Kalim Allah Jahanabadi

Haz'rat Shaykh al-Mashaykh Nizam ad-Din Awrangabadi

Haz'rat Shaykh al-Mashaykh Mawlana Fakhr ad-Din

Haz'rat Shaykh al-Mashaykh Ghulam Qutb ad-Din

Haz'rat Shaykh al-Mashaykh Nasir ad-Din Mahmud, *Kali-Shah*

Haz'rat Shaykh al-Mashaykh Muhammad Hasan Jili Kalimi

Morning Prayers

Haz'rat
Shaykh al-Mashaykh
Muhammad Abu Hashim
Madani

Haz'rat Pir-o-Murshid
Sufi 'Inayat Khan

Universel[6]

O maker, molder,
And builder of
The universe,
Build with your
Own hands
The Universel,
Our temple for
Your divine message
Of love, harmony,
And beauty.
Amen.

Dedication

This is not my body;
This is the temple
Of God.

MID-DAY PRAYERS

Invocation

This is not my body;
This is the temple
Of the heart.

Toward the One

Toward the One,
The Perfection of Love,
Harmony, and Beauty,
The Only Being,
United with all
The Illuminated Souls,
Who form
The Embodiment
Of the Master,
The Spirit of Guidance.

Salat[8]

Our most
Gracious sustainer,
Anointing savior
Of humanity,
We greet you
With all humility;
You are the first cause
And the last effect,
The divine light
And the spirit of guidance,
Alpha and Omega!

Your light is in all forms,
Your love in all beings ...

*Silently acknowledge
How God manifests
In all the people we love,
In each type of relationship.
For instance, as
Hazrat Inayat Khan
Has suggested –*
'In a loving mother,
In a kind father,
In an innocent child,
In a helpful friend,
In an inspiring teacher.'

Allow us to
Recognize you
In all your holy
Names and forms ...

*Silently remember
The various names by which
God and God's messengers
Are known in different
Religions.
For instance, as
Hazrat Inayat Khan
Has suggested –*

Gayatri

'As Rama, as Krishna,
As Shiva, as Buddha;
Let us know You as
Abraham, as Solomon,
As Zarathustra, as Moses,
As Jesus, as Muhammad.'

And in many others
Known and unknown
To the world!

We adore your past;
Your presence deeply
Enlightens our being;
And we look for
Your blessing
In the future!

O messenger of God!
You, whose heart
Constantly
Reaches upward,
You come to Earth
With a message,
When religion decays,
As a dove descending
From above,
Speaking the word
That fills your mouth,
As light fills the
Crescent moon.

Let the Star
Of the divine light
Shining in your heart
Be reflected in the hearts
Of your devotees!

May the message of God
Reach far and wide!
Illuminating
And making
The whole of humanity
Into a single family
In the parenthood
Of God!
Amen.

Remembrance

Recite eleven times:

May the message of God
Reach far and wide!

Nabi[9]

A torch in the
Darkness,
A staff during
My weakness,
A rock in the
Weariness of life,
You, my masterful guide,
Make Earth a paradise!

Mid-day Prayers

Your thought gives me
An ethereal joy;
Your light illuminates
My life's path,
Your words inspire me
With divine wisdom;

I follow
In your footsteps,
Which lead me
To the eternal goal!

Comforter of the
Broken-hearted,
Support of those
In need,
Friend of the
Lovers of Truth,
Blessed and
Masterful guide,
You are the
Prophet of God!
Amen.

Universel

O maker, molder,
And builder of
The universe,
Build with your
Own hands
The Universel,
Our temple for
Your divine message
Of love, harmony,
And beauty.
Amen.

Dedication

This is not my body;
This is the temple
Of God.

EVENING PRAYERS

Invocation

This is not my body;
This is the temple
Of the heart.

Toward the One

Toward the One,
The Perfection of Love,
Harmony, and Beauty,
The Only Being,
United with all
The Illuminated Souls,
Who form
The Embodiment
Of the Master,
The Spirit of Guidance.

Khatum[10]

O Perfection of love,
Harmony, and beauty,
Sustainer of heaven
And earth,
Open our hearts
That we may hear
Your voice,
Constantly coming
From within.

Disclose to us
Your divine light,
Hidden in our souls,
That we may know
And understand life
Better.

Merciful and
Compassionate God,
Give us Your great
Goodness;
Teach us Your loving
Forgiveness;
Raise us above
The distinctions
And differences
That divide us.

Send us the peace
Of your divine spirit,
And unite us all
In your perfect being.
Amen.

Remembrance

Recite eleven times:

Disclose to us
Your divine light!

Rasul[11]

Warner of
Coming dangers,
Awakener of the
World from sleep,
Deliverer of the
Message of God,
You are our savior.

The sun at the
Dawn of creation,
The light of the
Whole universe,
The fulfillment of
God's purpose,
You, the life eternal,
We seek refuge
In your loving
Embrace.

Spirit of Guidance,
Source of all beauty,
Creator of harmony,
Love, lover,
And beloved sustainer,
You are our divine Ideal.
Amen.

Universel

O maker, molder,
And builder of
The universe,

Build with your
Own hands
The Universel,
Our temple for
Your divine message
Of love, harmony,
And beauty.
Amen.

Dedication

This is not my body;
This is the temple
Of God.

OCCASIONAL PRAYERS

Iyayaki Blessing[12]

May the
Blessings of God
Rest upon you;
May God's peace
Abide with you;
May God's presence
Illuminate your heart,
Now and forevermore.
Amen.

Du'a[13]

Save me,
My sustainer,
From the earthly
Passions
And attachments
That blind humanity!

Save me,
My sustainer,
From the temptations
Of power, fame
And wealth
That keep us from
Your glorious vision!

Save me,
My sustainer,
From the souls
Constantly occupied
With hurting and
Harming others,
Who take pleasure
In another's pain!

Save me,
My sustainer,
From the evil eye
Of envy and jealousy
That falls upon
Your bountiful gifts!

Save me,
My sustainer,
From falling
Into the hands
Of the Earth's
Playful children,
Lest they use me
In their games,
And break me
In their ends!

Save me,
My sustainer,
From all manner
Of injury
Coming from
The bitterness
Of my adversaries,
And from the ignorance
Of my loving friends!
Amen.

Prayer for Peace[14]

Send your peace,
My sustainer,
Perfect and everlasting,
That our souls
May radiate peace.

Send your peace,
My sustainer,
That we may think,
Act and speak
Harmoniously.

Send your peace,
My sustainer,
That we may be
Contented
And grateful for
Your bountiful gifts.

Send your peace,
My sustainer,
That amidst our
Worldly strife
We may enjoy
Your bliss.

Send your peace,
My sustainer,
That we may
Endure all,
Tolerate all,
In the thought
Of your grace
And mercy.

Send your peace,
My sustainer,
That our lives may
Become a divine vision,
And in your light
All darkness
May vanish.

Send your peace,
My sustainer,
Our father
And mother,
That we,
Your children
On earth
May all unite
In one family.
Amen.

Nayaz[15]

Beloved sustainer,
Almighty God!
Through the rays
Of the sun,
Through the waves
Of the air,
Through the
All-pervading
Life in space,
Purify and quicken me,
I pray—heal my body,
Heart, and soul.
Amen.

Occasional Prayers

Nazar[16]

Sustainer of our
Bodies, hearts and souls,
Bless all that we receive
In gratitude.
Amen.

Prayer for Humanity[17]

O God,
Whose nature is
Mercy and compassion,
Whose being is peace—
Father, mother,
Creator, and sustainer
Of our lives—
Send Your peace on the
Whole of humanity,
And unite us all
In your divine
Harmony.
Amen.

Spirit
Of our souls,
Master
Of our minds,
Controller
Of our bodies;
We humbly offer
Ourselves as channels
For your love,
Light, and life,
That we may
Better serve you
And humanity.
Amen.

Light of all souls,
Life of all beings,
Healer of hearts,
All-sufficient,
All-powerful God,
Forgiver of our
Shortcomings,
Free us from all
Pain and suffering,
And make us
Your instruments,
That we may,
In our turn,
Free others from
Pain and suffering,
Imparting your light,
Your life, your joy
And your peace.
Amen.

Prayer for the Departed[18]

O God,
Source of
The universe,
The cause from
Whence we come,

Gayatri

The goal toward
Which we are bound,
Receive the soul of . . .
(say their full name)
Into your gentle arms.

May your loving
And merciful countenance
Heal *(their/his/her)* spirit,
And remove any burdens
(They/he/she) may yet carry.

Surround *(them/him/her)*
With your warm
And gentle light,
And elevate *(them/him/her)*
To *(their/his/her)* eternal
Inheritance.

Grant *(them/him/her)*
The blessing
Of Your most exalted
Presence.

May *(they/he/she)* awaken
From the dream
Of this life
Into the glorious vision
Of your splendor
And sunshine.

We thank you
With all of our hearts
For lending
(Them/him/her) to us
For this short season.

We will treasure
(Their/his/her) memory
And be grateful
All the days
Of our lives.
Amen.

Prayer of Healing and Blessing[19]

My Beloved
Sustainer,
Heal this spirit,
From all the
Wounds
Its heart
Has suffered
In this life
Of limitation
On Earth.

Purify this heart
With your divine light,
And send your mercy
Upon its spirit,
Your compassion
And your love.
Amen.

OCCASIONAL PRAYERS

Prayer for the New Year[20]

You,
Who abide
In our hearts,
Most merciful and
Compassionate God,
Sustainer of
Heaven and Earth,
We forgive others
Their trespasses,
And ask your
Forgiveness
For our own
Shortcomings.

We begin this New Year
With a pure heart
And a clear conscience,
With courage and hope;
Help us to fulfill
The purpose of our lives
Under your divine
Guidance.
Amen.

REMEMBRANCES

The Ten Remembrances[21]

I.
There is one God,
The only being;
Nothing else exists.

II.
There is one master,
The Spirit of Guidance,
Constantly leading
Its followers
Toward the light.

III.
There is one
Holy writing,
The sacred
Book of Nature,
The only scripture
That truly enlightens
Its reader.

IV.
There is one religion,
Unswerving progress
On the true course
Toward the ideal,
Fulfilling the
Life-purpose
Of every
Soul.

V.
There is one law,
The Law of Reciprocity,
Observed by a
Selfless conscience
Wedded to a sense of
Awakened justice.

VI.
There is one family,
The human family,
Uniting the children
Of the Earth,
Indiscriminately
In the parenthood
Of God.

VII.
There is one moral,
Love springing from
The transparency
Of the self,
And blooming
In deeds of
Loving-kindness.

VIII.
There is one
Object of praise,
Beauty that lifts
The heart
Of its worshipper
Through all of its aspects,
Seen and unseen.

IX.
There is one truth,
The true knowledge
Of our being,
Within and without;
The essence of all
Wisdom.

X.
There is one path,
The path of
Making the self
Transparent to the real,
Raising the limited
Beyond limitation,
The dwelling-place
Of all perfection.

The Three Objects[22]

I.
To realize and spread
The knowledge of unity,
The religion of
Love and wisdom,
So that triumphalism
In religion
May fall away,
The human heart
May overflow with love,
And all hatred caused
By distinctions
And differences
May be rooted out.

II.
To discover
The light and power
Latent in the
Human being,
The secret of all religion,
The power of mysticism,
And the essence
Of philosophy,
Without interfering
With custom or belief.

III.
To bridge
East and West
In thought and ideals,
Forming the
Universal Fellowship,
Where human beings
May meet
Beyond the narrow
Boundaries
Of tribal identity.

The Iron Rules[23]

I.
Make no
False claims.

II.

Remembrances

Speak not
Against others
In their absence.

III.
Do not
Take advantage
Of a person's ignorance.

IV.
Do not boast
Of your good deeds.

V.
Do not claim
That which belongs
To another.

VI.
Do not
Reproach others,
Making them firm
In their faults.

VII.
Do not spare
Yourself in the work
Which you must
accomplish.

VIII.
Render your
Services faithfully
To all who require them.

IX.

Do not
Seek profit
By putting someone
Else in straits.

X.
Harm no one
For your own
Benefit.

The Copper Rules[24]

I.
Consider your
Responsibility
Sacred.

II.
Be polite
To all.

III.
Do nothing
Which will make
Your conscience
Feel guilty.

IV.
Extend your help
Willingly to those
In need.

GAYATRI

II.
Use tact
On all occasions.

III.
Place people rightly
In your estimation.

IV.
Be no more
To anyone
Than you are
Expected to be.

V.
Have regard
For the feelings
Of every soul.

VI.
Do not
Challenge anyone
Who is not your equal.

VII.
Do not
Make a show
Of your generosity.

VIII.
Do not
Ask a favor
Of those who
Will not grant it you.

V.
Do not look
Down upon
The one who
Looks up to you.

VI.
Judge not another
By your own law.

VII.
Bear no malice
Against your worst
Enemy.

VIII.
Influence no one
To do wrong.

IX.
Be prejudiced
Against no one.

X.
Prove trustworthy
In all your dealings.

The Silver Rules[25]

I.
Consider duty
As sacred as religion.

Remembrances

IX.
Meet your
Shortcomings
With a sword of
Self-respect.

X.
Let not
Your spirit
Be humbled
In adversity.

The Gold Rules[26]

I.
Keep to
Your principles
In prosperity
As well as
Adversity.

II.
Be firm
In your faith
Through all life's
Tests and trials.

III.
Guard the secrets
Of your friends
As your most
Sacred trust.

IV.
Observe constancy
In love.

V.
Break not
Your word of honor,
Whatever may
Befall you.

VI.
Meet the world
With smiles
Through all the
Vicissitudes of life.

VII.
When you
Possess something,
Think of the one
Who does not
Possess it.

VIII.
Uphold your honor
At any cost.

IX.
Hold your ideal high
In all circumstances.

X.
Do not neglect those
Who depend on you.

INAYATI-MAIMUNI PRAYERS & REMEMBRANCES

Source of Time and Space[27]

Source of
Time and space,
Our sovereign
Father and mother,
Draw down to us
The great renewal,
A stream from
The infinite,
Attuning us to
Your timely intent.

Let wisdom flow
Into our awareness,
Awakening us
To foresight,
Guiding us to help
Instead of harm.

May every
Tool and device
Of human use
Be sparing
And protecting
Of your creation.

Help us to set right
All that we
Have debased,
To heal what we
Have made ill,
To care for and restore
What we have injured.

Bless the Earth,
Our home;
Guide us in how
To care for her
So we might live
According to
Your promise,
Days of heaven
Here on earth.

May all the beings
You have fashioned
Become aware of You
And the gift of being
You grant them
In every moment.

May we realize
The shaping
Of our lives,
And may everything
That breathes
Share breath
And knowing,
Delighting in the
One great breath.

Guide us in
The understanding
Of the art of partnering
With family, with friends,
And with neighbors,
New and old.

Aid us in dissolving
Old enmities;
May we come to honor,
Even in those
Whom we fear,
Your image and form,
Your light-dwelling
In their hearts.

May our star soon
Rise on the day
When your house
Will indeed be
A house of prayer
For all peoples,
Named and celebrated
In every tongue;
On that day
You will be known
As one with all
Cosmic life.

The Priestly Blessing[28]

May God
Bless you and keep you;
May God
Shine favor upon you;
May God
Countenance you,
And grant you peace.
Amen.

The Thirteen Aspirations of Faith[29]

I.
My God,
I aspire to
Perfect faith
In your
Infinite Light,
Issuing from the source
Beyond time and space,
Who, longing for
A dwelling-place
In the worlds below,
Compassionately contracts
Her radiant glory
In order to emanate,
Create, form, and effect
All that exists in
The universe.

II.
My God,
I aspire to
Perfect faith
In your oneness
With all of creation;
A oneness
Without a second,
A oneness that says,
All that exists

In the universe

Is called into being
According to
Your desire
In every
Moment.

III.
My God,
I aspire to
Perfect faith
In your intent
And purpose
In creation;
That the divine *he*
May become
Known to us
Through creation,
The divine *she;*
That we expand
This awareness
Until the worlds
Are filled with the
Consciousness of God,
As the waters
Cover the sea.

IV.
My God,
I aspire to
Perfect faith
In your unfolding plan,
In which all of us
May come to constitute
One consciously

Interconnected

And organic whole;
That every living being
May know that you
Are the one who
Constantly causes
Their existence.

V.
My God,
I aspire to
Perfect faith
In all the paths
Through which the
Holy spirit manifests
And reveals to us;
That all your
Manifestations are one,
Though called
By different names
Through time
And space.

VI.
My God,
I aspire to
Perfect faith
In the mission
Of each path
As an organ of
The collective being
That comprises
All existence;
That through
Your compassion

Gayatri

On all creatures
It be revealed to all
How integral
Each Message is
To the health
Of all the species
Of our collective
Being.

VII.

My God,
I aspire to
Perfect faith
In the reciprocity
Of your universe,
Which takes our
Impressions;
That everyone
Who does good
With their own life
Takes part in the fixing
Of the world,
And that everyone
Who uses that life
For negative purposes,
Likewise participates
In the destruction
Of the world;
That every action
Has an impact
On the rest of
Existence.

VIII.

My God,
I aspire to
Perfect faith
In Your perfect
Judgment;
That the amount
Of good
In the universe
Is greater than
The amount
Of negativity;
And that our
Entire movement
Through the chain
Of evolution
Is designed
To bring about
The fulfillment
Of your divine
Intention.

IX.

My God,
I aspire to
Perfect faith
In your traditions;
That the deeds
Of our mothers
And fathers
Inure to the benefit
Of their children;
That the traditions
Passed on

Contain within them

Inayati-Maimuni Prayers & Remembrances

The seeds of the light
Of redemption.

X.
My God,
I aspire to
Perfect faith
In your compassion;
That our prayers
Are heard and
Answered.

XI.
My God,
I aspire to
Perfect faith
In your holy
Presence,
Dwelling in
Our midst;
That all who
Show kindness
To living creatures
Also show kindness
To you.

XII.
My God,
I aspire to
Perfect faith
In your continuity;
That physical death
Does not terminate
The existence
Of the soul;

That there are

Innumerable worlds
In which souls
Reside.

XIII.
My God,
I aspire to
Perfect faith
In the fixing
Of the world,
And our part
In its awakening:
Possessing life,
Consciousness
And feeling,
Becoming a fitting
Vessel for the
Revelation of the
Divine will.

Notes

Morning Prayers

1. *Invocation:* An invocation composed by Pir-o-Murshid Inayat Khan, adapted here from "the temple of God" to "the temple of the heart," to emphasize going inward at the beginning of one's prayers. It is part of what is called 'The External Zikr.'

2. *Toward the One:* An invocation composed by Pir-o-Murshid Inayat Khan.

3. *Saum:* A prayer of Pir-o-Murshid Inayat Khan found in the *Gayan*, translated and adapted into modern, gender-inclusive English. In Farsi, *saum* refers to an 'opening recital,' and in Arabic, to a 'fast' or 'abstention.' Inayati Sufis recite this prayer at dawn, at the beginning of the day (during the fast period), so both the Farsi and Arabic meanings are appropriate. It is also recited at the opening of the formal Inayati gatherings.

4. *Pir:* A prayer of Pir-o-Murshid Inayat Khan found in the *Vadan*, translated and adapted into modern, gender-inclusive English. The Farsi word, *pir*, means 'elder,' and usually refers to a Sufi master.

5. *Silsila:* The official *silsila* of all the Inayati lineages up to their founder, Hazrat Inayat Khan, as verified by Pir Zia Inayat Khan.

6. *Universel:* A prayer of Pir-o-Murshid Inayat Khan translated and adapted into modern, gender-inclusive English. The words "our Temple" were added by his son, Pir Vilayat Inayat-Khan. 'Universel' is pronounced as in French.

7. *Dedication:* An invocation composed by Pir-o-Murshid Inayat Khan, used here as a dedication, to emphasize going out at the end of one's prayers. It is part of what is called 'The External Zikr.'

Mid-day Prayers

8. *Salat:* A prayer of Pir-o-Murshid Inayat Khan found in the *Gayan* translated and adapted into modern, gender-inclusive English. Some lines have been removed and used as examples. The Arabic word, *salat,* means 'prayer.'

9. *Nabi:* A prayer of Pir-o-Murshid Inayat Khan found in the *Vadan* translated and adapted into modern, gender-inclusive English. The Arabic word, *nabi,* means 'prophet.'

Evening Prayers

10. *Khatum:* A prayer of Pir-o-Murshid Inayat Khan found in the *Gayan,* translated and adapted into modern, gender-inclusive English. The Arabic word, *khatum,* means 'closing recital.'

11. *Rasul:* A prayer of Pir-o-Murshid Inayat Khan found in the *Vadan,* translated and adapted into modern, gender-inclusive English. The Arabic word, *rasul,* means 'messenger.'

Occasional Prayers

12. *Inayati Blessing:* A blessing composed by Pir-o-Murshid Inayat Khan, traditionally given by cherags (universalist Sufi ministers) at the end of the Universal Worship service. A melody for it was composed by Pir Puran Bair.

13. *Du'a:* A prayer of Pir-o-Murshid Inayat Khan found in the *Gayan* as 'Dowa,' translated and adapted into modern, gender-inclusive English.

14. *Prayer for Peace:* A prayer of Pir-o-Murshid Inayat Khan translated and adapted into modern, gender-inclusive English.

Notes

15. *Nayaz:* A prayer of Pir-o-Murshid Inayat Khan found in the *Gayan,* translated and adapted into modern, gender-inclusive English. According to Inayat Khan, *nayaz* refers to a kind of "feminine chivalry."

16. *Nazar:* A prayer of Pir-o-Murshid Inayat Khan found in the *Gayan,* translated and adapted into modern, gender-inclusive English. The Arabic word, *nazar,* means 'glance' or 'seeing.'

17. *Prayer for Humanity:* A prayer of Pir-o-Murshid Inayat Khan translated and adapted into modern, gender-inclusive English.

18. *Prayer for the Departed:* A prayer of Pir-o-Murshid Inayat Khan translated and adapted into modern, gender-inclusive English.

19. *Prayer of Healing and Blessing:* A prayer of Pir-o-Murshid Inayat Khan translated and adapted into modern, gender-inclusive English.

20. *Prayer for the New Year:* A prayer of Pir-o-Murshid Inayat Khan translated and adapted into modern, gender-inclusive English.

Remembrances

21. *The Ten Remembrances:* These ten remembrances, usually called, 'Ten Sufi Thoughts,' were originally composed by Pir-o-Murshid Hazrat Inayat Khan in 1914 as seven "Sufi Teachings." Later, in 1917, he published a revised list of ten "Sufi Teachings," which, in turn, underwent revisions until 1923, from which time we have the "Ten Sufi Thoughts," as they are used today by most Inayati Sufis. Sharif Graham has suggested that the word "teachings" may still have had too much a flavor of "doctrine" to it, and was thus abandoned in favor of the word, "thoughts." This new version was created to clarify and make the language both gender inclusive and

more accessible to modern readers.

22. *The Three Objectives:* The Three Objects were formulated by Pir-o-Murshid Hazrat Inayat Khan and have been translated and adapted into modern English to clarify them and make the language both gender inclusive and more accessible to modern readers. They may be connected to three similar objects of the Theosophical Society.

23. *The Iron Rules:* "The Iron Rules" were composed by Pir-o-Murshid Inayat Khan and are found in the *Vadan*.

24. *The Copper Rules:* "The Copper Rules" were composed by Pir-o-Murshid Inayat Khan and are found in the *Vadan*.

25. *The Silver Rules:* "The Silver Rules" were composed by Pir-o-Murshid Inayat Khan and are found in the *Vadan*.

26. *The Gold Rules:* "The Golden Rules" were composed by Pir-o-Murshid Inayat Khan and are found in the *Vadan*.

Inayati-Maimuni Prayers & Remembrances

27. *Source of Time and Space:* A prayer originally composed by Pir-o-Murshid Zalman Sulayman Schachter-Shalomi, included in the book *Earth Prayers,* later revised in his lifetime into the present version by Pir Netanel Miles-Yépez.

28. *The Priestly Blessing:* This blessing found in Numbers 6:24-26 is here translated by Pir Netanel Miles-Yépez.

29. *The Thirteen Aspirations of Faith:* Thirteen affirmations originally composed by Pir-o-Murshid Zalman Sulayman Schachter-Shalomi, based on 'The Thirteen Principles of Faith' of Maimonides, reflecting a more kabbalistic worldview, later revised in his lifetime into the present version by Pir Netanel Miles-Yépez, included in *Foundations of a Fourth Turning of*

Notes

Hasidism: A Manifesto.

Hazrat Inayat Khan was born in Baroda, India, on July 5th, 1882. A master of Indian classical music, he gave up a brilliant career as a musician to devote himself full-time to the spiritual path. In 1910, he followed his master's direction to go to the West to "spread the wisdom of Sufism" in the United States, England, and throughout Europe. For a decade and a half, he traveled tirelessly, giving lectures and guiding an ever-growing group of Western spiritual seekers. In 1926, he returned to India and died there the following year, on February 5th, 1927. He is entombed in the precincts of the *dargah* of Hazrat Nizam ad-Din Awliya'. Today, the universalist Sufi teachings he spread continue to inspire countless people around the world, and his spiritual heirs may be found in every corner of the planet.

Pir Netanel Miles-Yépez is the current head of the Inayati-Maimuni Order of Sufism. He is the author of *In the Teahouse of Experience: Nine Talks on the Path of Sufism* (2020), and the Modern Reader's Editions of Hazrat Inayat Khan's *The Bowl of Saqi* (2021) and *Gathekas* (2021).

www.ingramcontent.com/pod-product-compliance
Lightning Source LLC
Chambersburg PA
CBHW020244010526
44107CB00002B/92